Backyard Chickens

A GUIDE FOR BEGINNERS

NEW
HOLLAND

MICHELLE TEMPLIN

This edition published in 2014 by New Holland Publishers
London • Sydney • Cape Town • Auckland
www.newhollandpublishers.com • www.newholland.com.au

First published in 2011 by Michelle Templin.

The Chandlery Unit 114 50 Westminster Bridge Road London SE1 7QY
1/66 Gibbes Street Chatswood NSW 2067 Australia
Wembley Square First Floor Solan Road Gardens Cape Town 8001 South Africa
218 Lake Road Northcote Auckland New Zealand

A catalogue record of this book is available at the British Library and at the National
Library of Australia

ISBN: 9781742574516

10 9 8 7 6 5 4 3 2 1

Publisher: Fiona Schultz
Project editor: Jodi De Vantier
Designer: Tracy Loughlin
Production director: Olga Dementiev
Printer: Toppan Leefung Printing Limited

Follow New Holland Publishers on
Facebook: www.facebook.com/NewHollandPublishers

Contents

Introduction

I owned my first chickens as an adult, eight years ago. My partner had very covertly purchased a breeding trio of Light Sussex from the suburbs to kick off our flock. We had just moved to acreage and wanted to do the self-sufficiency thing as much as possible. So in went the vegetable patch and up went the chicken coop.

I look back and think I was rather 'spoilt' to receive such a lovely pure breed trio as my introduction to chickens. Within a month of owning this delightful band of three, I was hooked. I spent my weekends watching their antics, and fell in love with them. I was fascinated with the way Roger (Sussex being an old English breed, I thought it only appropriate that they had slightly pompous sounding English names) would protect his ladies Diana and Cynthia from screeching overhead birds—

and sometimes even me. He was the perfect gentleman when it came to down to the 'business end' of breeding, and soon I was charged with fertile eggs and an incubator.

Within a month I had to have more. Three was just not enough! I headed down to my local produce store. The choice was pretty easy—Isa Browns, or Isa Browns. Later visits revealed the 'black ones' and 'white ones'. Of course, we had to have some of them, just for the visual stimulation.

It's all a learning experience, one full of laughs and sometimes tears. I remember the first time I heard the now familiar high-pitched screeching sound of a girl about to lay an egg. I thought they were under attack! I rushed down to the pen, armed with a shovel ready to deal with a fox. All I found was a girl pacing about trying to decide which laying box was best suited to her bottom that day.

My interest and passion continued to grow, and so did my flock and breeding efforts. I realised that there was a keen following for backyard chickens as part of the trend towards greener living. 'Chicks in the City' was born—a hobby farm weekend business run with the help of my partner and daughter.

At the 'peak' of Chicks in the City, my breed list included Anconas, Australorps, Light Sussex, Buff Sussex, Barnevelders, Plymouth Rocks, Silver Laced Wyandottes, Welsummers, Pekin Bantams and Silkies. All on my five-acre property. I mustn't forget to mention my beautiful 'working girls'—my Isa Browns. I kept about thirty girls and two boys to assist in breeding these perfect backyard layers.

All of them would free range in cordoned off areas to make sure that the pure breeds would stay pure. We backed on to a river, so my feathered family had quite the idyllic setting to forage about in.

I tell this recount in past tense, as I am now a backyard chicken farmer as well. We moved back to the suburbs for work, but I wasn't about to let my ladies go completely. Our block is only 600 square metres in an inner city suburb. But just because you don't have acres of land, you shouldn't miss out of the experience of raising chickens.

If you haven't already embarked on the journey of owning chickens, I hope that you are inspired to after reading this book!

Michelle

Chapter One

Why Keep Backyard Chickens?

It's certainly not a new 'hobby', but it is definitely a growing one. As society becomes more and more conscious of being eco-friendly and self-sufficient, keeping a small flock of chickens is no longer something only for large land-owners.

Suburbanites everywhere are waking up to the delights of a freshly laid egg for their weekend breakfast.

Here are some common reasons why people keep backyard chickens:

- Golden yolk fresh eggs daily—most agree they taste better than cage eggs sold in the supermarket.
- Fertiliser 'on tap' for your vegetable garden—four hens will produce 40kg/6 stone of high quality organic fertiliser per year.

- Garbage compost for your household scraps.
- Chemical-free bug and weed control.
- Children can observe the full life cycle of our feathered friend's right from the incubating of the egg.
- Chickens make for an amusing, interactive and rewarding pet. They are very social and will provide hours of entertainment with their backyard antics.
- You are doing something for the good of an animal—accessing your egg supply in a non-caged, humane environment.

All you need now is a bit of information on chickens, so you know what to expect, what you will need and what to look for when selecting your girls.

Chapter Two

Covering the Basics

Do you want a chick, pullet, cockerel, cock, point of lay, rooster or hen? Like most animals, there are different names for genders and ages.

Chicken—A chicken is either a hen or a rooster.

Chick—Day old to 7 weeks, often 'unsexed' (meaning no idea if it's a boy or girl) mainly because they are too young to tell.

Pullet—(pronounced 'pull-it') A young female chicken who hasn't started laying. These girls tend to be sold around the 16 week or older mark. You will pay more for them as they are approaching the age where laying commences.

A young Plymouth Rock Pullet. Not only is she very small in stature, but her comb and feathers are still developing.

'**Point of Lay**'—or POL for short, and typically advertised for sale using this acronym. Pretty much as the name says, girls who are at the point where they will start laying. Perfect for impatient folk who want the eggs ASAP.

Hen—A female chicken anywhere from the age of laying onwards.

Cockerel—A rooster (cock) under the age of 12 months.

Cock—Another name for rooster, a boy over the age of 12 months.

This Australorp was just about to enter her first season of laying. Her size was quite developed already, as they are a heavy breed. The redness of her comb is indicative of her age and preparation to start laying.

12

This fine boy was the pride and joy of my flock. My prize-winning Australorp Rooster—Ignathio.

Bantam—A bantam is not a breed of chicken as such, it's just the smaller version of a full sized breed. Much like getting a 'miniature poodle', you just get a smaller, more petite, version of the bigger breed. There are, however, 'true bantam' breeds, meaning there is no bigger version.

Parts of a chicken

Spurs do exist on female chickens and can sometimes be quite pronounced. Identifying spurs is often a way of determining gender, so the presence of a pair on a female can be quite confusing.

Combs can be straight or rose comb, depending on the breed. Wyandotte's tend to have rose combs.

The crop on a chicken can get large and bulbous when they have just finished eating. New chicken owners often mistake this for a tumor or something equally scary. It will normally go down by morning. This can be particularly pronounced in greedy little chicks.

A straight comb on an Australorp.

A rose comb on a Gold Laced Wyandotte

How to handle a chicken

First-time chicken handlers often end up with a face full of flapping wings and a few scratches as a nervous girl protests being caught and held. There are two ways to hold a chicken. Which method you use depends on how comfortable the girl is with being held.

For ladies who are used to being handled, you can catch them by gently restraining the wings against their body. Then carefully lift the girl to your chest, freeing up one of your hands by continuing to restrain the wing against your chest. This also frees up a hand to gently pat and calm your girl.

For the feistier girls who aren't used to human contact, the method used by seasoned handlers is better suited, as it also restrains the feet and helps to prevent scratching.

Face the girl towards you and put your index finger through the legs facing the rear end of the bird.

Grip one thigh with your thumb and the other with your three loose fingers.

The keel of the bird should either rest in the palm of your hand or along your forearm, depending whether it is a bantam or standard sized chicken.

Are all eggs fertile?

No. Like all species, female chickens do need a male chicken to make a fertile egg.

A rooster will mount the female, then dovetail their rear feathers, thus aligning their vents, and the sperm sack is transferred into the females vent.

When does a hen start to lay eggs?

If you want eggs straight away, you will need to buy a 'Point of Lay' (or older) hen. Be wary of buying a hen that is too old, and thus closer to her end of laying days. There are visual signs that a hen is coming into the age of egg laying, but the easiest way to know is to ask the person you are buying her from.

A sure way of knowing you are getting a girl who hasn't yet entered her egg laying years is to buy a pullet. She will be around the 16-week mark, and laying starts with most breeds around 24–28 weeks. You will have a little bit of a wait, but at least you are guaranteed that she is a young bird.

Sex of a Chicken

Chicks are very difficult (near impossible) to visually determine gender, unless they are sex-linked. In some pure breeds it can take up to six months to work out if you have a boy or a girl. Sex linking occurs when a specific breed of hen is mated with a specific breed of rooster. The product of which is a chick who is able to be determined visually as a male or female, typically by the colouring or markings of the feathers.

However, as chicks get older, there are some signs that help you work out what gender you are dealing with:

- Boys will have larger, redder combs and wattles sooner than girls. This can sometimes be evident very early on.
- Boys hold themselves more upright
- Boys have more defined 'erect' tail feathers
- Girls do tend to be smaller in stature than that of their male counterparts of the same age
- Girls are more 'rounded' and not so upright in their stature
- Boys tend to have thicker legs than the girls
- Boys will start crowing (always a giveaway)
- Boys will start showing territorial aggression towards each other

Some breeds have specifics indicators as well. For instance, Plymouth Rock boys tend to have bald elbows.

Age of a Chicken

Aside from a baby chick being very obviously a baby chick, this can be difficult. There are certain breed specific visuals that allow you to age a chicken. Signs of older age are a bit easier to see:

- Faded combs
- Legs look quite scaly and old
- Saddle feathers can look worn from constant rooster mounting

A good way to indentify a pullet in the common backyard breed—the Isa/Hyline Brown—is by the yellow of their legs. A young girl who hasn't started laying will have legs that are a very vibrant yellow. This is actually the pigments that form the egg yolk. So as she reaches laying age and older, her legs fade to a white colour.

Just because a chicken is small in stature, it doesn't mean she is young. Bantam breeds, even fully grown, are very small birds.

Moulting and Brooding

Moult

A hen will moult to revitalise herself for the laying season ahead. This will mean a reduction in egg production, and her feathers will fall out, typically about the head and neck. Growing new feathers requires additional protein, so she acquires this by not putting it into eggs.

Don't fret that your gorgeous show-quality pride and joy now looks like something rescued from a battery farm. She will regain her glamorous appearance, but it's hard to say how long that will take. You may still even get the occasionaly egg if she is having a 'partial moult'.

Commerical layers such as the Isa of the Hyline will not moult. They have been bred specifically for laying. Unfortunately, this does mean that the poor old girl does not get the recuperation offered by a moult, and it shortens her lifespan significantly.

Roosters may also experience feather loss during the moulting season.

Broody

This is the term given to a hen that is determined to hatch a chicken from an egg by sitting on it—no matter what. Sure, it's not even fertile, but she doesn't realize that! She will spend her days—yes days—sitting on the egg doing her bit for the chicken race. She will neglect her food and water, the need to stretch her legs—and her duty to lay more eggs!

As you will note further on in the characteristics of different breeds, some are more prone to bouts of broodiness than others. This can be beneficial if you would like to experience hatching fertile eggs. Silkies are often used to hatch and raise chicks for other breeds. They are very careful and are natural mothers.

To prevent broodiness, remove the eggs from the nesting boxes as quickly as possible. To stop broodiness isolate the girl for a couple of days from the other hens and the ability to get near eggs. It sounds harsh but it does often break the broodiness.

Chapter Three

Things to Consider Before Buying Chickens

There are so many positives to owning backyard chickens, it's tempting to rush out and buy your first mini flock. However, like all domestic animals, there are things to consider:

Neighbours

It is very rare to find a rooster in a suburban backyard, due to the handy crack of dawn wake up call they offer daily. As a backyard chicken farmer in suburbia, you would probably have little need for a rooster anyway.

If you did want to experience hatching your own eggs, you can purchase fertilised ones, thus negating the need for the male. Backyard chicken breeders have some very ingenious creations that they have come up with to house their boys overnight in order to prevent the crowing disturbance. If you would like a rooster, you should check with your local council, as most have very strict rules on the keeping of roosters.

Your girls are not totally mute, they will make a gentle clucking as they go about their daily business of fossicking for food. When they lay an egg this clucking can get a tad louder, but in terms of noise pollution in the suburbs—it's hardly up there! There are far more annoying noises for neighbours to worry about.

Children

Not so much a consideration, but rather assurance that chickens are typically docile pets and rarely show aggression—except to each other to establish a pecking order. Some breeds are more likely to 'interact' with your family (refer to breed list showing temperaments).

Showing your children how to properly handle chickens as you would any animal, to protect the chicken from accidental harm is a good idea. The younger your girls are when you purchase them, the greater the chance of them being more relaxed around humans.

With many of my girls that I have raised since chicks, if I simply sit on the ground, it is an invitation to them to jump up on my knee. Silkies, in particular, are great for small children, as there is an obvious great size match. On one occasion, I visited a customer with a home delivery and saw a very content silkie being pushed about in a doll's pram!

Space

Do you have enough? This is probably more about how much space you have for each chicken. Refer to the section on housing for the recommended dimensions for chicken living areas.

Safety

Unfortunately there is a lengthy list of predators that would enjoy your chickens as much as you do. When thinking of a suburban neighbourhood, consider possible access points for dogs and even cats.

There are a number of residential suburbs that are not immune to foxes. Flying predators such as crows and magpies have been known to swoop and injure bantam breeds; so if possible, an enclosure with a wire/netting roof is perfect. As suburbs start to merge into forest or bush land, snakes are quite common—and you aren't the only one who enjoys a nice fresh egg. While probably not a big an issue as it is for rural chicken owners, it's best prevented by collecting your eggs regularly.

Escape routes

Just as predators can get in, your girls can get out. In fact, some breeds in particular are excellent Houdini's. If your backyard fences are not particularly high, you may want to clip your girl's wings.

Time

Chickens are fairly self-sufficient creatures, but they do rely heavily on fresh water and feed. If you are someone who enjoys frequent weekends away, you may need to make sure you have a friend who can drop by and top up the supplies when you're gone.

Local Government and Council Rules

Check with the conditions of your local government or council before buying roosters for a backyard breeding project.

Buying Unsexed Chicks

Everyone loves the cute fluffy baby chicks, but to get them at this age you run the risk of not knowing if your little one is a boy or girl (unless sex linked). In some pure breeds, gender isn't apparent until 4–6 months. If you want to start the chicken journey from the very beginning, it's best to have a 'Plan B' ready for the boys you may end up with. Placing a classified advertisement offering a rooster for free often attracts the interest of those who rear boys for the pot.

Your Other Pets

I've mentioned neighbourhood dogs and cats, but what about yours? Unfortunately very few dogs live in harmony with chickens. Also keep in mind that dogs dig. If you have a small dog, don't be lulled into a false sense of security. My adorable little ShihTzu was a very accomplished serial chicken killer!

Sometimes you can be very fortunate with the interaction of your girls and other pets. The body language in this picture says to me that the poor old dog knows exactly who the boss is in his backyard!

The Age of the Chicken

Day old to four- to five-week-old chicks require a source of light for warmth. They can't be put straight outside in a coop. If you buy little ones, make sure you have some form of a 'brooder' where they can do some growing before moving to the coop. Also be aware of the dangers of putting in young chickens with fully grown ones. Establishing the pecking order can turn nasty.

Pecking order is pretty clear here! I did have four other nesting boxes mind you, but clearly this one is 'Australorp ONLY'.

Chapter Four

What Breed is Best for You?

Which chicken is best suited to you, your space and environment?

Hybrid Layers and Pure Breeds

There are two 'types' of chickens—Hybrid Layers and Pure Breed Chickens.

Hybrid Layers—Isa Brown and Hyline Brown

Production chickens have been 'engineered' by crossing breeds to achieve mass egg production. You have probably heard of the most common one, as it was no doubt recommended to you as a great backyard layer—the Isa Brown.

This girl is a 'hybrid' cross-breed chicken, which means she actually can't even call herself a breed. She was developed in France, and the 'ISA' of her name stands for *Institut de Selection Animale*. The ISA Brown is a cross between a Rhode Island Red and Rhode Island White.

Another hybrid layer is the Hyline Brown. She is hard to distinguish from the Isa, and most backyard breeders and produce stores will sell Hylines as Isa's. Not for any untoward reason, but mainly because Isa is the name most people recognize. The egg production of a Hyline is on par with the Isa.

Pro—Great egg production, not likely to moult (go off the lay).

Con—These little girls condense years of egg laying into two to three years. They don't get a natural break to rejuvenate like pure breeds (hence no moult). This takes a toll on them and they only live for two to three years.

Pure Breeds

With the exception of the Isa/Hyline Brown, the table below lists pure breed chickens that are readily available to backyard chicken owners. Cross-breeding is still possible, but you end up with a cross breed—not a hybrid. Pure breeds are not as commonly available as the production layers, and you will rarely see them in a local produce store.

Pros—They live longer than the hybrids, so better for families who get attached to their girls. Lifespan differs per breed, but five to six years is average. As much as I love my 'working girls', it has to be said that pure breeds are far more interesting to look at in terms of patterns and feathering.

Cons—You won't get an egg a day, more like every third or fourth. These girls will moult and may have a tendency to go broody.

Eggs

Not only is the amount of eggs you require important when deciding on a breed, but also of interest is the colour of the eggs. Totally an asthetic requirement, different breeds do lay very different coloured eggs.

Araucana's lay beautiful blue/green eggs. Marans lay a very deep brown egg. For more information on the colour egg each breed lays, refer to the Appendix for a full Breed List.

The dark brown, almost copper appearance of Maran eggs.

Araucana blue egg shown against a traditional white and brown.

29

Chapter Five

Where Will You Put Your Chickens?

You've decided which breed you want, so now it's time to get your backyard ready for the new arrivals. Note I do say 'arrivals' because chickens are a flock breed. This means they need at least one mate.

Are your chickens able to 'free range'?

It's not often possible in suburbia to let your girls out of their coop to wander the backyard at their leisure. Perhaps you can opt for a few hours a day when you're home to keep an eye/ear on things. For most backyards, an enclosure (or run) is the better solution. If you are able to let your girls out for a wander, keep in mind that they might not realise that your beloved vegetable garden is in fact not their local supermarket. One of the backyard chicken owners I spoke to had a great way of looking at the balance between chicken and vegetable garden—'if they can reach it, it's theirs!'

Equipment you will need

The coop (house) is the biggest requirement, so we have dedicated the next chapter to it. There are a few other items you will need as well:

Drinker—Water plays a very important role in a chicken's health and ability to produce eggs. A fresh, clean supply is a must. You could use a cut-down bucket, saucepan, or something else you have laying around your house. However, keep in mind that chickens scratch about, so an uncovered water supply often ends up with the fly-offs of a girl throwing dirt about in search of something tasty. They also tip things over as they attempt to perch.

Your local produce store will have a few options, but by far the most popular and practical is the 'green and white' drinker. These regulate the water flow themselves with gravity, so as your ladies drink, the water keeps topping up (until empty). They come in various sizes, and have a handle which allows you to hang them from above. By doing this, you help keep the dirt and everything else out that your girls are prone to shoveling in there. Just ensure it's at the right height for them. This can also be achieved by placing the drinker on pavers or other, to elevate it from ground level.

Be sure to clean drinkers regularly, as they will accumulate algae. This then creates harmful bacteria. And wash them regularly, even daily, in the warmer months. The best way to remove any germs the algae may leave behind is by leaving the empty drinker in the full sun to dry.

*A collection of drinkers and feeders in various sizes
for sale at a produce store.*

Feeder—As per the drinker, you can use anything you have around the home. One important aspect in food availability for your girls is their ability to waste it, or scatter it about. When they do, their leftovers attract mice. Mice carry germs and also attract other predators. Feeders are also available in different sizes from a produce store.

This 'top down' view of a feeder shows the divisions that assist in keeping a bit of order at feed time.

Straw/wood shavings—This is a must for lining the nesting boxes. Ladies require a bit of comfort to do their thing. It will require changing often, so getting a bale lot at a time is a good idea. It also provides excellent insulation. Personally, I prefer straw over wood shavings, as the shavings are easily kicked out of the box and, in terms of reusing them on the garden, wood shavings can be too acidic. Straw can also be placed on the floor of the coop for that added bit of comfort. The other main benefit is that the chickens will inevitably poop on it, so when you clean out the coop, dump the whole lot on your garden beds easily for fertilised mulch.

Optional Extras

Here are a few things that are certainly useful, but by no means 'vital' for the homecoming.

Worming solution—Chickens should be wormed quarterly. Using the seasons as a reminder is a handy idea. It's available at produce stores, and the directions for dosage are on the bottle. You simply add it to the drinking water. Don't do this on hot days, as your girls may drink more than usual and the intake of the solution could be harmful.

Apple and garlic cider vinegar—This is a natural pick-me-up for your girls and some people use this as a natural alternative to worming. During the colder months, I add it to my girls' water, as it helps ward off flu's and general 'run down' effects. I am also quick to dose them up if they start to look a little off-colour. The cider assists in the drying up of mucus.

Egg 'stunt doubles'—Not their technical name, but they do the same thing. To encourage your girls to lay, and to work out what the nesting box is for, place a couple of fake eggs in them.

Lice dusting powder—Dirt baths can only work so well. If you have an outbreak of lice, you may need extra help. It's also useful as a preventative. Instructions are on the container and it's available in produce stores.

Shell grit—This is crushed-up shells rich in calcium to assist the girls in creating stronger egg shells. Place a small amount separately, but nearby, to their food.

Bringing Home Chicks

Baby chicks require a source of heat until they are approximately four to five weeks of age. If you are in the middle of a harsh winter, this could be longer. This setup is known as a 'brooder'.

If you aren't planning to hatch on a regular basis, or have just purchased chicks as a once (or maybe twice) off, then a simple brooder creation is all you will need.

Make Your Own Brooder

A brooder is the name of the small, heated enclosure used to accommodate chicks. It offers protection and warmth, just as the mother hen does. It's easy enough to make your own:

A **large plastic storage container** can be easily washed and reused after use. You won't be using the lid that comes with it, but when the little ones start getting a little restless and flighty, place something like an old fridge rack over the top.

Add to this a **desk lamp with a flexible arm**. This will provide the heat source. Better still, use that type of lamps with a clamp on the end for attaching to bed heads. These are great as they clip on to the edge of the container. The flexible arm feature allows you to adjust the level of the lamp, thus increasing and reducing the degree of heat. The correct temperature for chicks

A Silkie chick.

in a brooder is 33°C/92°F in the first week, then reduce by half a degree each day to about 24°C/75°F by week 5.

Line the container with **paper towels**. These are the best for the chick's feet, as it allows them to grip as they get used to walking. Newspaper is slippery, and sawdust can get in their eyes and cause a nasty infection. It's also very easy to swap out when cleaning the brooder.

Make sure you have a chick drinker. These are smaller and prevent the chicks from drowning. Pebbles can also be used in open dishes of water. For the food, I simply cut down an old takeaway (or similar) container. Sprinkling the food on the floor and making a tapping action in it with your finger is a great way to teach the little ones how to eat.

 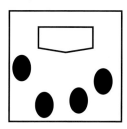 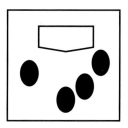

| Chicks too cold— crowding around light | Chicks too hot— spread right out | Best temperature— near light but not crowded |

This is the set-up just described.

Raising Chicks More Than Once?

If you plan to hatch chicks often, then you may require a more 'professional' set up. Once again, I'd mention that just because you are in the suburbs, that shouldn't stop you from experiencing the joys of breeding chickens. Obviously you just have to find a way to sell on your new arrivals—or buy yourself some acreage!

As previously mentioned, buying fertilised eggs negates the need to keep a rooster in suburbia, so hatching chicks and growing them to sell is a very viable hobby in your backyard.

If this is the case, you may want to explore the more permanent options available for brooders. The following set-ups are not always readily available in local produce stores, so you may have to order online from a poultry specialist provider.

The actual brooder itself can still be a make-it-yourself job, and over the years I have heard of some excellent ways people have made perfect solutions relatively cheaply, or even for free.

As per the container/tub, you are looking for something that has high sides to prevent mischievous chicks from escaping. Also remember, these cute little babies will learn to fly as they get bigger.

For the actual brooder, some ideas include:

- Building a square structure using fence palings or plywood to a height that allows you to get in and out to clean it easily, while not allowing escapees.
- An old swimming pool outer structure—the metal or hard plastic type (just pay attention to the height).

- The hexagonal hard cardboard enclosures that fruit shops use for apples, etc. These need to be cut down a bit, as they tend to be too high.
- An old wooden wardrobe laid down on its back, with the back removed.

As you can see, the possibilities are many. The equipment you may need to purchase is more along the lines of the lighting/heating solution.

The more chicks you have, the more lights you will need. Everyone needs the ability to get their fair share.

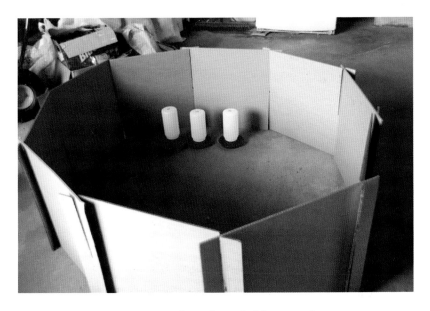

Photo courtesy of www.happylittlehomestead.com.

Chapter Six

The Coop (House)

The Coop

During the day your girls will want to forage about in the run or free range, but at night they will need somewhere safe and dry to live.

They have some requirements for their new establishment:

Safe and lockable—We've already covered predators, so you know why their house needs to be secure. 'Windows' should have chicken wire covering them; the door should be able to be locked up. Not necessarily a padlock job, but some mechanism that doesn't allow a very curious fox to paw its way inside. In some areas you may also need to think 'snake proof'. Aviary wire is the best solution.

Stopping predators digging their way in—In addition to the safety measure above, you also have to consider the threat posed by predators that dig. Nothing comes between a hungry fox and a chicken. The speed at which a fox can dig his way into a coop is alarming, and the results are catastrophic, and something no one wants to wake up and find. There are a couple of solutions to prevent this problem:

- **Trenches**—if your coop is a permanent fixture, then digging a foundation around the perimeter is a good way to prevent digging predators. Dig a trench 30cm/12in deep and 10cm/4in wide, and fill with concrete preferably. Pavers or bricks are another option. Then make sure that the coop is absolutely secured to the foundation.
- **'Skirting'**—this is a solution for movable coops, but can also be used with permanent coops. It involves nailing a skirt of mesh around the bottom outside of the coop. This skirt must extend at least 40cm/16in and be securely pegged into the ground. The effect is that a fox would have to dig an extra 45cm to get under the wire to reach the inside of the coop.
- **Mesh on the bottom of the coop**—I'm not a fan of this solution, as when the chickens are in the coop (in particular a mobile coop) for an extended period of time, their natural habit to scratch meets with wire. It's a very safe solution, but I can't help but see it as cruel.
- **Electric fencing**—another very viable solution, but perhaps not ideal in a backyard. Especially where there are other pets and children.

Ventilation—Especially important in the hot summer months. When referring above to 'windows' I didn't mean glass. More like a wooden flap that can be held open to allow for air in the stifling hot evenings. Just as importantly, the windows should be able to be closed to prevent cold draughts in the winter months. Preventing mould is also important and a good air flow will assist in this.

Accessible—The girls will need to lay eggs as the moment seizes them, so an easy way of coming and going back into the house to lay is paramount. This is referred to as a 'pop hole'.

Laying boxes—Girls prefer privacy, partial darkness and the feeling of being safe and 'confined' when laying. One laying box per four girls is recommended, the size of which should be

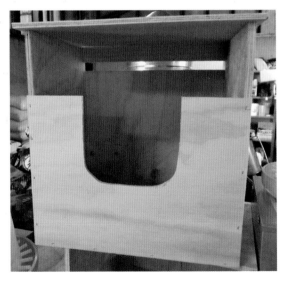

A laying box.

30 x 30 x 30cm/12 x 12 x 12in. Make sure it is clean at all times. The options for lining the box include straw, wood shavings, shredded paper or pine needles. Be warned—girls are very fussy. If they don't like the offerings, or if it is in the least bit too dirty, they will start laying where they decide is suitable. While this may provide for an interesting egg hunt, it really impacts your egg supply as you have no idea how long the eggs in your latest discovery have been sitting there. Straw/hay holds the shape of a nest well and girls love the familiarity.

Perch—Chickens sleep standing up on perches. People tend to think of a perch as being cylindrical, like a broomstick. This is not the case, as that is quite uncomfortable for a chicken to grasp on to, and can cause foot problems. Instead, a perch should be A rectangular piece of wood with rounded edges, 4–5cm/1½-2in wide. Allow a length of approximately 20cm/8in per bird.

The lowest perch should be 45–60cm/17½–23½in from the ground. If you have the need for multiple perches, don't place them directly under each other.

Easily cleaned—Here's a fact: chickens poop. A lot. So you're going to need to be able to get in their house easily to clean it. Straw will need to be changed and that marvellous organic fertilser removed to throw on your gardens.

Lighting—Like all living things, light is important for the health of chickens. It also creates a preferable laying environment and aids in the protection against predators.

Location and environment—Consideration must be given

Note the extended beam that allows the tractor to be picked up and moved.
Two rear wheels are also a common feature.

for extreme heat and cold during each season. Also be aware of rainy seasons. If the coop is a permanent structure, then you'll need to take note of trees for shade, rainwater run off and raising the floor off the direct ground.

Placement of drinker and feeder—Ideally these should both be off the ground. Being natural scratcher and foragers, your girls will not think twice of kicking dirt, shavings or other into the water you just freshly filled up. They will also make a serious attempt to spread their feed in every place known to man and chicken within their coop. Placing both the drinker and feeder at the height of their back is ideal. This can be achieved by suspending the feeder from a beam by a rope or by placing it on bricks.

Movable—This is an option for those with very little space. A chicken 'tractor' is a house on wheels, which can be moved around the yard to allow your chickens who aren't able to free range to have fresh grass. Below is a common design, the 'A Frame'. Note the handles to pick up and move.

How big does the coop and run need to be?

The best answer to this comes down to how much space you have available and some common sense. There are guideline dimensions listed below, but anyone should know what overcrowding looks like, and how to avoid it.

The following measurements are PER CHICKEN:

Full Size Chickens
- Coop—0.4 sq metres (or 4 sq feet)
- Run—0.7 to 0.9 sq metres (or 8–10 sq feet)

Bantams
- Coop—0.3 sq metre (3 sq feet)
- Run—0.6 to 0.7 sq metres (6–8 sq feet)

These are minimum measurements. Think about quality of life when selecting just how many hens to get for the space you have.

More About 'The Run'

We briefly touched upon the run when discussing free-range options. Basically a run is an enclosed area where the chicken is able to scratch about freely. It's a bit of extra space outside the coop for during the day. It can be just four sides or, in some instances, it may include the wire/netting overhead to protect from flying predators. This is a particularly good idea for bantam breeds or chicks that have just left the brooder.

They are easy enough to make and, better still, the materials are often found in recycling depots or junkyards. This can be said for the coop as well. Chickens aren't into aesthetics, just safety.

Make sure the wire you use has small holes if you have young chicks or bantams. It's also a good idea to grab a bit of roofing iron or shade cloth from the recycle depot as well to provide shade from the summer sun.

If your girls are in the run on a full-time basis, and there is room, placing a tub of dirt inside is useful. Girls love a dirt bath and it is beneficial for them in terms of alleviating boredom and removing external parasites.

Your Options and Where to Buy

A lot of people love the idea of building their own coop and run out of recycled material. It adds to the eco-living aspect of having chickens. However, not all of us were blessed with handyman skills. Buying ready-made or do-it-yourself kits form are the solution.

David of Belconnen, ACT built this coop from brand new building material. It's his own design— obviously he is pretty handy with a saw and drill

Coops and runs for self-assembly are readily available online for purchase. However, I have heard and seen some horror stories when it comes to the cheaper imported models. They aren't really made for being out in the weather, and warp easily, which creates problems trying to keep the girls safe. I tried purchasing a few and 'improving' them by using a good quality weather-shield paint and adding a 'skirt'.

If you want a better quality one, produce stores often have a local builder who has seen an opportunity for a bit of extra pocket money and supplies them with a quality solution.

By far the best option I have seen to date is an all-metal, fully insulated walk-in coop manufactured by a builder who designed it for himself, being a fellow chicken lover. I have one and I'll list the pros and cons of it, and the others, below:

Building Your Own

There seems to be no limit to people's creativity when it comes to modifying something they already own, or can get cheaply, into a very useful coop. Old metal A-frame swing sets are popular, dog kennels—you name it—if it's suitable, use it! Here is an excellent example. This suburban family turned the kids' old cubby house that was no longer used into an amazing coop and run. Hubby extended the roof out, and enclosed a safe area for a run. The elevation of the cubby provide safety, and extra space underneath for the girls to do their thing. Best of all—it looks great!

With a few modifications, this cubby house has become the perfect chicken 'house'.

Pros

- If recycling material—excellent for the environment.
- This activity can really add to the whole experience of owning chickens—get the whole family involved!
- Can be purpose-built to fit into your backyard perfectly.

Cons

- Just be sure that hubby's/dad's DIY handywork is secure!

Imported Varieties

Pros

- Priced cheaply and found online for purchase easily.
- Very easy to clean, most have slide-out trays to clean the droppings from. Just hose them down!
- Easy to assemble
- Very light-weight timber
- Visually they are nice to look at—all very neat
- Variety of sizes and styles available to suit individual backyards

Cons

- The timber is cheap and tends to warp, making doors and other safety features difficult to close over time.

- Often requires additions such as better designed perches, lockable pop doors and run.
- While they are light enough to move about, they tend to fall apart if moved too often.

Buying Local from Produce Store

Not found at every produce store, just ones where there is a local builder or handyman who has placed them there for sale. Obviously there would be a big variance in design and materials for each one.

Pros
- In my experience, these tend to be sturdy in structure and made of good material.

Cons
- These aren't cheap to buy—not so much a con, but commonly found to be the case. So save your pennies!

The 'Taj Mahal' (in my humble opinion)

To make my dream chicken coop, I contacted a local builder who turned my design and requirements into this walk-in coop. So, it rates as my favourite, but I will explain why:

Pros

- Aluminium frame that will not rot, rust or succumb to the weather.
- Walk-in height—perfect for avoiding sore backs.
- Able to be moved around easily—on wheels and lightweight.
- Absence of wood deters knowing predators determined to get their meal.
- Insulation—This material reacts with either condition to keep my girls comfortable all year round. It's fully non toxic.
- Easy to assemble, can be delivered flat packed.
- All recommended measurements have been used in terms of space.

Note the rear wheels for easy moving—perfect if your girls can't free range.

This is the view of the internal area from the lockable rear door. Fully insulated, and plastic nesting boxes are easy to remove for cleaning. Photos courtesy of www.coolcoops.com.au

- Dimensions—H180cm/6ft x W120cm/4ft x D270cm9ft.

Cons

As per the locally made coop, this is not cheap. However, if you are looking for a coop that will last forever, you will more than get your money's worth as an investment.

Catering to Your Climate

The outside elements can be particularly harsh, and given that your girls are outside pets—they are exposed to all extremes. Whether it be scorching summers or freezing winters, your girls need protection from both ends of the weather scale. Here are some tips to ensure that you provide the best possible care for all seasons.

Caring for Chickens in the Heat

Water is the key element to keeping healthy chickens all year round, regardless of the weather. However, in summer it becomes even more vital as external factors such as evaporation come into play.

- Try to keep the water supply in a spot that is shaded all day long
- Check the water as often as possible to make sure it's clean and hasn't all been consumed and/or evaporated
- During extreme heatwaves, add ice to the supply, as girls won't want to drink warm/hot water.
- Ventilation in the coop is very important. In some parts of

the world, the summer heat in the evenings is relentless, and three or more feathered ladies cramped into a small coop won't make for the most comfortable conditions. Just make sure that any openings are covered by strong wire mesh to prevent predators entering.

- **Location**—I have known many a chicken owner to bring their girls inside to a cool place in the house, such as a garage when the thermoter tips 40°C/104°F. If this isn't an option, make sure your girls have access to a well-shaded area to escape the direct sun.

Caring for Chickens in the Cold

Once again, water is a big challenge for the chicken owner in the extreme cold. I was faced with frozen taps outside each morning when performing my daily maintenance. Larger scaled chicken owners will often run electricity to their henhouse and use warming methods to keep the water supply unfrozen. As a backyard chicken owner, this probably isn't practical. Instead you can try:

- Keeping 'back up' waterers inside the house where it is warmed and swap them out during the day as required.
- Fill the waterer with warm water and add a chunk of ice, allowing the water to slowly cool over the course of a few hours
- If you do have a safe way of running electricity out to the coop, there are a variety of heating devised that you can sit a waterer on top of.

- Ventilation is also important in the cold, as the litter (straw, etc) needs to be kept dry. Wet litter can lead to nasty respiratory infections in your girls. Allow the litter to build up, that is, add new litter to old, obviously ensuring that the old is not filthy. Turn the litter regularly. A drying agent can also be used to prevent moisture.

- Heating is often advised against in coops. The main reason for this is safety. Girls have the tendancy to fling their litter about and if this lands on a heater of some description, it could catch alight and start a fire. Try to make sure that a pop door or window can be opened to allow natural sunlight to enter the coop. If free-ranging is possible, the girls will gravitate to a warm sunny spot to spend their time.

- Create a path for free-ranging girls through snow. No matter how dire the conditions are outside, chickens will insist upon performing their daily foraging. Excessive snow on their feet can lead to frostbite.

- Remain watchful for signs of frostbite on wattles and combs. Any areas of your girls that aren't covered in feathers are susceptible to freezing weather.

Chapter Seven

What Do Chickens Eat?

If your girls are able to free range, they will scratch about for tasty worms, bugs, grass and pretty much anything they can find. Chickens eat both vegetables and meat.

You will need to by them feed, even if they free range. Exactly what type is dependent on their age:

Age	Feed
Day old to 6-week-old chick	Chick starter crumble
7 weeks to 16 weeks	Chick grower crumble
16 weeks to adult	Layers mash, layers pellets, scratch mix

Chick starter and grower crumble is medicated to assist in preventing a nasty intestinal parasite known as Coccidiosis.

Layers mash comes in a mash (finely crushed/pulverised powder) form that requires water to be added to it. In winter, I use hot water when mixing it up, to provide a warm treat for the girls.

Layer pellets are available either on their own, or in a mix commonly referred to as Layer Mix. They are a pelleted form of layers mash.

Scratch mix is another good feed to spread about for them to scratch about in, as the name implies. It's made up of grain, corn, seeds and other goodies. It's not recommended to be the only feed used, as it contains no layer pellets.

A variety of brands of each are available at produce stores. They are sold in large 20kg–30kg/3–5st bags, and once opened will attract mice and rats from far and wide. Buy a well-sealing tub/bin to store the food as you use it.

Scraps

Let's not forget one of the major benefits of having chickens—household scrap disposal units. Your girls will recycle just about anything for you. But never give them onion, avocado, potato peelings or rhubarb leaves.

Treats available at produce stores include bags of cracked corn, wheat and meal worms. These are treats though, and shouldn't form the crux of their diet—as much as they'd love you!

A healthy fresh treat that also serves as a form of entertainment can be easily made by stringing together some vegetables. Using something sharp, like a screwdriver, pierce holes through various vegetables such as a broccoli stem, carrots, cauliflower, zucchini/courgette. Use a piece of string to then thread through the holes, as if you were making a necklace. Then tie the creation somewhere just a smidge below head height (that's chicken head!). The girls will peck away for ages and the natural momentum of the treat will be both a fascination and a challenge for them.

How Much Should I Feed my Chickens?

There isn't an exact answer for this question. A number of uncontrollable variables come into play such as how much food is taken by vermin and other freeloading animals—other birds mainly! Weather and where they are at in their laying cycle will also contribute to how much they eat daily.

You don't want to waste too much food by oversupplying your girls, but a feeder should be full all day—allowing them to come and graze as required. If your girls free range, they are able to supplement their diet. However, if they are in the coop/run 24/7, they will obviously require you to provide all their food. The amount of scraps you provide will also lessen their interest in the actual chicken feed you give them.

The longer you have your ladies, the more you will observe about their eating habits. You'll see how much they plough through in a day, what foods they will not eat and what they can't get enough of. There is a recommendation of 120g/4oz per chicken per day, however, as mentioned, it really depends on other factors.

They may even show you a time of the day when they prefer to eat. There is a lot of benefit in not overfeeding, as the leftovers will bring rats and other unwanted guests to their area. Also be sure to remove uneaten/unwanted scraps, as they can attract pests.

Providing fresh feed daily as much as possible is important. Water is more vital, and you will be changing this daily, so adding the feeding task is not a big deal.

Chapter Eight

Chicken Health

Chickens will get sick; they are no different to humans and other pets. Here are some preventative steps you can take to help them.

- **Buy healthy birds**—Ask if the bird is vaccinated and when you bring her home don't put her in with your existing brood straight away.
- **Watch your chickens**—Observe your girls and their actions. Look out for changes in their behavior, feather pecking (bullying) and any out of season moults. The comb is also an excellent indicator of health. A bright red comb shows excellent health and egg laying ability. The lighter it becomes has a direct relation to the amount of eggs produced. During a moult, it will be a much paler pink.

- **Worming**—This should be done at least four times a year. It's easy enough to do, just buy worming solution for poultry from your produce store, add it to their clean drinking water as per the dosage on the bottle, and they will sip at it as they do with their normal water.
- **Lice and mite dusting**—Dusting powder is also available at your produce store and should be used as a preventative for your girls. Apply it well under their wings and around their vent area, as this is a common nesting ground for the cretins. Lice are pale yellow, fast-moving and about 1–6mm/0.03–0.2in in size.
- **Water**—Water, water, water. Especially in summer! Girls won't drink warm water, so try adding ice cubes to their drinker to keep it cool. It must always be clean and the drinker itself should be washed thoroughly regularly to prevent the build-up of algae.
- **Heat**—Keep a watchful eye on your girls during hot summer days for any signs of heat stress. Make sure they have plenty of water and shade. It may even be worthwhile bringing them into the house (or garage) if it is cooler. Putting ice cubes in their water to help keep it cooler is great for extreme heat.

Common Illnesses in Chickens

- **Lice**—Lice spend their entire lifecycle living on chickens. They lay their eggs at the base of feathers, particularly around the vent area.

- **Mites**—Unlike lice, mites will live in the surrounding environment as well as on a chicken. As such, when treating your chickens for mites you must also treat the areas around them such as the nest, perches and cracks and gaps in the coop. The most common mite is the 'Red Mite'. It comes out at night and feeds on the blood of the bird. Visit your produce store for specific products designed to eliminate this pest. A natural alternative is a mix made from 1 cup of cooking oil (any type) and 1 tablespoon of dishwashing liquid. Add 4 tablespoons of this mixture to 475ml/16fl oz of water in a spray bottle. Spray daily for a few weeks during an outbreak.
- **Scaly legs**—This is a condition caused when mites bore into the scales on the legs, making them swollen and 'crusty'. Left

Scaly Leg—photo courtesy of indianapublicmedia.org

untreated it can cripple a bird. Treatment involves 'smothering' the mites with Vaseline®.

- **Coccidiosis**—an internal parasite that causes symptoms such as diarrhoea, blood stained droppings, dehydration and death.
- **Worms**—can be detected in the droppings of chickens. Prevent by using worming solution. Roundworms are contracted by eating insects such as grasshoppers, earthworms and beetles. Other visible signs include paleness around the face, listlessness and diarrhoea.
- **Marek's Disease**—this is a particularly nasty illness and results in death. The most obvious symptom is paralysis, typically in the wings and legs. If affecting both legs, one will be splayed forward, the other to the rear. If signs of paralysis are present, don't immediately assume it's Mareks. Other causes include spider/snake bite, leg strain. Sadly, most

A Plymouth Rock struck with Marek's. Note the classic splaying of legs.

chicken experts agree it is more humane to cull a bird with Marek's than attempt to treat it.

- **Crop Bounding**—the crop of a chicken can become impacted, which means feed forms a ball in the crop. This can be treated by gently massaging the crop to break down the ball. Feeding chickens shell grit help prevents this problem.
- **Feather Pecking**—this can be caused by boredom, overcrowding and stress.
- **Blood on egg shells**—young birds starting to lay, or older birds laying large eggs.
- **Soft-shelled eggs**—this can be caused by lack of calcium, so ensure the girls are getting enough feed made for layers. It can also be the first few eggs of a new layer.
- **Egg peritonitis**—symptoms include swollen abdomen and the pecking of own undercarriage feathers. It is caused by yolk fluid leaking from the oviduct and ovaries into the abdominal cavity. The yolk can then get into the blood stream and poison your bird and it can get laid down in the liver, causing an enlarged liver and liver damage. Unfortunately recovery from this nasty is not likely.
- **Egg binding (or egg bound)**—this is when the egg is stuck inside the chicken. Causes include lack of strength to expel the egg, old age and lack of calcium.
- **Sniffles and wheezing**—this could be as harmless as a slight common cold from the change in seasons, to something more serious such as a respiratory infection.

Symptom Reference Chart

Symptom	Possible Cause
Major paralysis	Marek's Disease, snake bite, spider bite, mould poisoning
Legs paralysed	Marek's Disease, algae poisoning, botulism
Feather eating	Deficiency in nutrition, typically protein
Swollen face	Sinusitis, flu (around eyes particularly)
Rough scaly legs	Scaly leg mite
Blood in droppings	Coccidiosis
Foamy droppings	Internal parasites
Weak-shelled eggs	Dietary deficiency, specifically calcium

Natural Preventatives

Various edible flowers and plants provide a free natural medicine for chickens. These can be planted around the coop or run, to allow for snacking as they choose. Benefits include gut cleansing, prevention of internal and external parasites, insect repellants and energy and immunity boosts.

Nasturtium   Comfrey

Nasturtium—Great all-round medicinal herb with antiseptic and antibiotic benefits.

Comfrey—This is great for your chickens and your organic garden. Chop it up and feed it to your girls to assist in boosting protein.

Wormwood and Tansy—Not for eating, but rather grown around the chook pen to assist in repelling insects. You can also dry it, chop and scatter it throughout the coop.

Nettle—Boiled and the liquid added to your girls' mash—perfect for the colder months. Nettle is an excellent natural wormer. It also assists in egg production.

Garlic/garlic chives—Like nettle, a very effective natural wormer. Good all-round pick me up.

Yarrow—Terrific digestive aid.

Peppermint—Planted around the coop to encourage girls to eat and walk on the plants. Assists in eradicating both internal and external parasites.

Dandelion—Good for boosting the immune system.

Tansy

Wormwood

Yarrow

Garlic chives

GARLIC CHIVES
Allium
tuberosum

Chapter Nine

Buying Your Chickens

The time has come! You have chosen your breed after careful deliberation, the coop and run is ready, you have the food—so now all you need are the chickens.

Hybrid layers are readily available all year round, due to their egg production. You will find them to purchase: at your local produce (fodder) store, in your local paper or from a breeder in the area.

Locating pure breeds is not as easy. Due to the moult, breeding is seasonal. Even then, laying efforts are influenced by:

- Episodes of broodiness
- Decrease in daylight hours
- Stress or a nasty incident, such as a fox attack
- The colder weather as winter sets in
- Seasonal changes

Chances are you won't be buying from a produce store when purchasing pure breeds; you will deal directly with a breeder. You can ask to be put on a waiting list or in an order book if you are really keen to secure your special girl.

You can also try online poultry forums, as they have classifieds. Given breeding is weather/seasonally dependant, you can sometimes source a breed from another state where the conditions are different to where you are.

To find a breeder:
- ask at your produce store
- search online poultry forums
- check the local paper
- ask at a poultry club in your area

Bringing your Chickens Home

How do you bring your new girls home? As a breeder, I was always appreciative of people who arrived with their own carrying solutions. A large cardboard box with flaps at the top to be sealed to prevent escapes is perfect. Air vents are easily cut into them.

A standard medium to large pet carrier used for dogs and cats is also ideal. Accidents can be hosed out of it easily. If you are unsure of how to safely handle your chicken, ask the person you are buying her from to give you a demonstration. Placing your new chicken in a box or cage will unsettle your girl and make her flightier than usual.

Once home, place your new arrivals in their readily prepared coop. Leave them in there for a couple of days, just to become familiar with her new environment before any free ranging. This will encourage their return on their first day of freedom when dusk falls, leaving you only to lock them up. Chickens really do 'come home to roost'.

Chapter Ten

Hatching Your Own Chicks

There is nothing quite as amazing as watching the egg you placed under a broody hen or in an incubator 21 days earlier start showing a tiny little beak pecking its way out.

It's a terrific learning experience for children and adults alike. The whole family will be vying for front row seats around the incubator when you start to hear little chirps from within the eggs when they are due.

You don't have to miss out on this experience because you don't have a rooster in your backyard flock. Fertile eggs are sold by breeders and incubators can even be hired.

Ingredients

You will need:

- Fertile eggs
- An incubator or a broody hen
- A special torch for 'candling' the eggs (not vital but a great addition to the whole experience—it lets you see inside the eggs at two points during the incubation
- Water
- Patience—it's only 21 days but it feels like forever waiting for those little babies to arrive!

Method

Incubating

As mentioned, this can be a broody hen. Silkie's are perfect for this role, as they are good little sitters and will lovingly care for the new chicks even if they don't resemble her in the slightest. The hen will do as she knows how, like all species it is ingrained in her. She will sit and sit, shuffling the eggs about gently to make sure they get the movement required for the process. As the hatch time approaches she gets even more diligent in her 'sit in', making sure the final days conditions are just right for her new additions. Letting a broody hen do all the work really does leave you very little to do. When you see her take to her nest, it's best to provide a spot for her away from the other chickens so she can do her thing safely and uninterrupted. It also protects her eggs, and later on chicks, when she does take that rare moment to stretch her legs.

Viewing spots can be a little difficult with a mother hen, unlike an incubator which can be set up in the house and usually has clear windows for everyone to keep a close on the progress until the final exciting day arrives.

This is one of my hatches in action. I call this incubator 'old faithful', as I get the best results from it. It does have an auto turner for the eggs, but I find I get more successful hatches by manually turning. That's why there is a 'M' (morning) and 'N' (night) on each egg, to remind me when they need turning, and which have been turned.

Collecting the Eggs

As a backyard chicken 'farmer', chances are you won't have a rooster, so this means your eggs will not be fertile. Contact a local breeder or check the online forums (they have classified sections) to source some fertile eggs. Like 'normal' eggs, they are often sold by the dozen, or in the case of pure breeds, individually.

A breeder will have taken care to store the eggs suitably for your use. That is tip down, rotated 45 degrees each day, and cleaned of dirt or feathers. They store them at room temperature to collect enough to make the dozen or amount requested.

Power up your incubator 24 hours before you are due to set the eggs. This allows you to get your temperature and humidity settings perfect before placing the eggs inside.

When handling the eggs, always make sure your hands are clean. Eggs have tiny pores (through which the chicks breathe), so they are susceptible to germs being transferred inside, which can kill the embryo. When you bring the eggs home, allow them to sit for 24 hours before placing them into the incubator.

Three Key Factors to a Successful Hatch

Heat	Humidity	Turning
Maintaining a constant temperature is VITAL to your hatch. Fluctuations, both lower and higher, can be the key point of failure. As with humidity, refer to the instructions that come with your incubator, but a general rule of thumb is to keep the temperature at 37.7°C/99.86°F.	Humidity allows the chick to remain moist enough in the egg to move about and ultimately break free at hatch time. Keeping water topped up in your incubator is the way to achieve this. Day 1 to 17 = 40–50% Day 17 to Hatch = 70%	Eggs must be turned regularly to prevent the yolk from settling to one side and to exercise the egg embryo. When you turn the egg, the embryo is exercised by turning in the shell until its head is upright. TIP—Mark your eggs on each side with a 'M' and a 'N' to remember which side to turn each morning and night.

The Steps

1. **Turn on your incubator** and set the temperature and humidity to the levels specified by the manufacturer. If it says 37.5°C, follow that advice rather than the common guidelines noted in the table. To achieve the required humidity, the instructions will often refer to the actual water tray that is to be filled.

2. After your incubator has been running for 24 hours at the desired temperature and humidity levels, **place your eggs** gently in the space allocated. Remember to have marked them if you are manually turning them. (some incubators have an auto turn tray)

3. Mark the day that you do this as **Day 1** on a calendar.

4. **Turn the eggs** once in the morning, and once at night, preferably with a 12-hour gap in between. Rotate them 180 degrees, tip to base, as compared to rolling them side to side.

5. **On Day 5** you can perform your first egg candle. As always, make sure you hands are clean, turn off the lights in the room and holding the egg tip down, place the egg candling torch over the base. This will create an 'x-ray' like effect on the egg, and what you are looking for are tiny blood lines. They look like veins running through the egg. This is a sign of fertility. Remove any eggs that don't show these signs.

6. Continue to **turn the eggs** twice a day until Day 17.

7. **Day 17** is an important day. It's time to candle the eggs once again. You will see something very different inside now. The

shapes of the chicks are actually visible, and if you look carefully you can even see them moving slightly. Once again, remove any eggs that have not progressed.

8. Day 17 is also known as '**lockdown**'. It's time to stop turning the eggs, and leave things be. If you have been using an auto egg turning tray, remove the eggs from it and take it out of the incubator. Make sure your water levels are topped up to Day 17 levels. Again, refer to the instructions, as they will often advise to fill an additional tray. Extra moisture at this stage is important for the chick to assist in her hatching process. We don't want her getting stuck to the egg shell!

9. Keep an eye on water levels, and temperature (as always). Try making a handy little contraption that allows you to feed water into the incubator without actually taking the

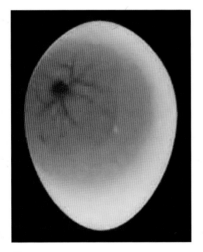
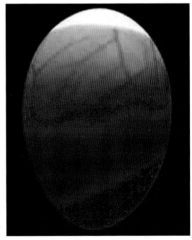

Day 5 Candling

Day 12 Candling
(Note the airsac)

76

lid off (through an air vent). Increasing the water levels will not increase the level of humidity. To do this you must increase the surface area of the water, which means filling an additional 'well' in the tray.

10. **By Day 20** you should start to hear 'pipping'. This is the sound of the chick pecking at the shell. You will see noticeable cracks appearing in the eggs. This is a very exhausting time for a chick, and the process from first peck to breaking out can be hours. It is often advised to never assist a chick who appears to be struggling over a long period to hatch. However, it can also be done successfully, and it's very hard to sit back and watch a little one doing her best getting nowhere after many hours.

11. **Day 21** should see all chicks hatched. Don't be disheartened if your first and even second attempt at incubating has less than favorable results. There is a science to the process, and every incubator is different.

12. Leave the chicks in the incubator for the **first 24 hours** after hatching. They need to dry out, and the heat inside the incubator is perfect for this. Take this time to prepare your brooder to the correct heat. Don't worry about food and water for the little ones at this stage as they have received enough sustenance from the yolk inside the egg to last them through this period.

13. Make sure you **clean and disinfect your incubator** thoroughly before using it again. It can carry nasty germs onto the next batch.

Other Important Things to Remember

Outside room temperature—Don't place your incubator in a part of the room that gets full sun or a draught. Outside temperature will have a significant effect on the inside temperature in the incubator, and spikes and lulls can be devastating to a hatch.

The ability to crack their way out by making an almost perfect circumference break never ceases to amaze me!

Ventilation—The instructions that come with your incubator hopefully show you where all the vents are. They may also direct you to have one closed if required until Day 17. This varies from machine to machine. Just remember, the eggs have to breathe, so don't forget this aspect when you are preparing your machine for incubation.

Keeping records—If you plan to incubate more than once, or maybe even just as part of a learning experience for the kids, keep records. Monitor things such as:

- Source of the eggs
- Number of eggs set
- Number fertile on Day 5
- Number of Eggs that chipped but didn't hatch
- Number of eggs that didn't chip
- Number of healthy chicks
- The temperature and humidity each morning and evening

Obtaining an Incubator

Incubators aren't cheap, and if you are intending to only use it once or twice, then it's a cost that you might not be able to justify. Try asking around to see if you can borrow one. There are some breeders who hire them out. If you think it is worthwhile buying your own, produce stores will often stock them. Do some research on better brands and think about how many eggs you intend to hatch at one time. Incubators range in egg capacity, starting at 3 and going up to 42 for home hatching.

When Things Go Wrong

Like anything, you learn from your mistakes and by keeping records and reading the instructions that come with your incubator carefully, you stand a good chance of successful hatch rates.

Getting an idea of the age of the embryo when it ceased to progress is always a good indicator of when things went wrong. Then you can go back to your records and try to find a cause. To determine timing, study the size of the air sac:

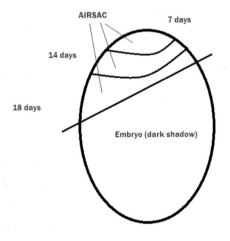

AIRSAC

7 days

14 days

18 days

Embryo (dark shadow)

The following table may assist in diagnosis:

Problem	Cause	Suggestions
No blood rings on Day 5 candling	• Infertile eggs • Eggs too old or dirty • Embryo died early, either before incubation or 1–2 days earlier	• Eggs should be no older than 14 days • Rough handling of egg and/or temperature extremes just after setting
Slight blood rings in most eggs	• Improper egg handling just before setting • Incorrect temp just before or after setting	• Eggs to be stored correctly • Check for temperature 'spikes' in incubator
Many dead immature chicks	• Improper egg turning • Incorrect temperature • Insufficient oxygen	• Eggs to be turned twice a day • Check temperature settings and correct for next hatch • Full ventilation may be required. Never cut off air flow.

Problem	Cause	Suggestions
Many chicks fully formed in shell with only some hatch 1 or more days early	• Temperature too warm	• Reduce temperature slightly for next hatch
Many chicks fully formed in shell with only some hatching one or more days late	• Temperature too cool	• Increase temperature slightly for next hatch
Many chicks fully formed in shell with only some hatching on expected date	• Humidity incorrect • Incubator opened too often during hatch • Insufficient oxygen	• Check air sac. If too large, increase humidity. If too small, decrease humidity.
Chicks fully formed but none hatched	• Temperature too extreme • Sudden and lengthy temperature change at hatch time • Insufficient oxygen	• Check accuracy of thermostat and thermometer. • Check air vents are open

Chapter Eleven

Chatting to Suburban Chicken Farmers

When I first started providing chickens and supplies to suburban residents, I really enjoyed being given the opportunity to look at their set-ups first-hand and, later, hearing from them about the experiences they were having as new backyard chicken farmers.

I contacted a few of them when writing this book, as I wanted to share their stories. Here is a collection:

Kate, Katrina, Tom and Jack

Ages of children: 5 and 7

Q: How many chickens do you have?

A: 15 (initially promised that I would only have 3 max!)

Q: What breeds do you keep?

A: Buff Orpington, Transylvanian Naked Neck, Pekin Bantam, Frizzle, Silkies, Plymouth Rock, 2 x rescue caged hens (Rhode Island Reds)

Q: How long have you had chickens at your current home?

A: 2 years

Q: Did you have them previously at this home?

A: No

Q: Who is the main caregiver to the chickens?

A: Kate, who works part-time.

Q: What made you decide to get chickens?

A: I have always loved them and have fond childhood memories of spending time with my grandparents on their property. We love the fresh, free range eggs. The educational experience (life cycle) for my children and I love the sound they make. We also wanted to be role models for our kids in regards to not supporting battery hen factories.

Q: What, if any, are the cons of having chickens in the suburbs in your opinion?
A: None that I can think of. Our neighbours already had them, and we also spoke to our other neighbours to give them a heads up, they had no concerns and were also considering them. We have two roosters (Pekin and Frizzle) and they sleep in a night box so they don't disturb us all with their 5am wake up calls. They crow a handful of times during the day and feedback from the neighbours (who don't have a rooster) love the sound and say it's nostalgic of being on a farm. You do need to be aware of mice control, but we've had no major issues.

Q: What are the pros of having chickens?
A: They make great pets, they're surprisingly friendly, the kids enjoy picking them up and love throwing them scraps. They keep our compost heap down as they love to scratch through it.

Q: How much space in your yard is available to the chickens?
A: We have a large pen along the fence but they're able to free range around the yard most days. We love having them out; they greet us at the back door waiting for food. Visitors love seeing them happy and content with so much space.

Q: Do you have other pets? If so, how do they interact with your chickens?

A: We have two dogs (pug Herman, rough collie Harry). Dogs love the chooks, they sniff around the pen and everyone eats together with no dramas.

Melanie, Greg, Hannah and Grace

Ages of children: 3 and 12

Q: How many chickens do you have?
A: Three

Q: What breeds do you keep?
A: We have Arabella Araucana, Beatrice Barnevelder and Sylvie Coronation Sussex.

Q: How long have you had chickens at your current home?
A: 3 months

Q: Did you have them previously to this home?
A: No

Q: Who is the main caregiver to the chickens?
A: Greg, who works full-time

Q: What made you decide to get chickens?
A: My youngest loved the chooks at her Grandma's when we went to stay at Christmas time.

Q: What, if any, are the cons of having chickens in the suburbs in your opinion?

A: None that I can think of.

Q: What are the pros of having chickens?

A: I really enjoy having them around in the yard; they are fun to watch as they peck and scratch.

Q: How much space in your yard is available to the chickens?

A: They have an enclosed yard under the trampoline in addition to their coop and we let them out when we're likely to be home most of the day.

Coll, Mike, Jack and Finn

Ages of children: 12 and 14

Q: How many chickens do you have?
A: Six

Q: What breeds do you keep?
A: We have Arabella Araucana, Beatrice Barnevelder and Sylvie Coronation Sussex.

Q: How long have you had chickens at your current home?
A: 3 months

Q: Did you have them previously at this home?
A: No

Q: Who is the main caregiver to the chickens?
A: Coll, who works four days a week. The boys help out when asked.

Q: What made you decide to get chickens?
A: Originally we thought it important that we learn to become more self-sufficient and I needed a new project. I spent a lot of time researching the ideal coop and most productive layers but ended up choosing the breeds believed to be gentle layers (they are) and which I thought looked great (they don't really

lay enough eggs as my Faverolles are poor layers). Our quest for self-sufficiency is somewhat hampered by my desire for the garden to be aesthetically pleasing as well as productive.

Q: What, if any, are the cons of having chickens in the suburbs in your opinion?

A: I am very conscious of the proximity of my neighbours and worry when the girls make a lot of noise (like when they are thinking of laying an egg, when they have laid an egg, when someone else has laid an egg, when I step outside or when they find themselves separated from the gang) but the only neighbour who has ever commented was positive and said he loved hearing them and thinking 'there's another egg' (not necessarily so but I don't tell him that).

I do not sleep in as late on the weekends as I used to because I know the girls will be desperate to get out and about. They used to make a racket if I didn't get up at first light to let them out but they don't do that anymore.

Although it only takes a few minutes twice a day, I am diligent about 'scooping the poop' to avoid odours. It's not hard or time consuming but neglecting this duty will spoil a hot, still evening outdoors.

Q: What are the pros of having chickens?

A: I know I should say eggs, but really, I don't get that many and I wouldn't be without the girls even if they never laid. They are such great company. I love pottering in the veggie garden with my 'chookies' following me and chatting continuously. It's very calming. They are funny and strangely smart. Their wonderful company and antics (even with few eggs) more than compensates for any cons.

Also, chicken poo is a great fertiliser.

I get up and enjoy the mornings with them instead of sleeping in. And I have met some interesting people who share a love of chickens.

Q: How much space in your yard is available to the chickens?
A: They have a coop with an attached run where I feel confident that they are safe from foxes or other predators when there is no one home. The coop (sleeping/laying) area is 1.5 x 1.5m and the run is 3 x 1.5m.

Q: Do they free range?
A: They 'free range' whenever someone is at home. They are out until it's time to leave for work and again in the evening as soon as the boys get home from school. Three days a week I am home and then they remain out most of the day. They have 2 kinds of 'free range': when we have visitors they are confined to a strip of land 1.5–2m wide and running along three borders of the backyard, around 40m2. This allows us to entertain without needing to warn guests to check their shoes before entering the house and keeps them safe when we are mowing the lawn. Most

of the time they have free range of the backyard (except the raised vegetable beds which have low, about 2 feet, plastic nets around them). The yard is 10 x 15m. I am not sure if this area would be considered true free range but they appear happy and we still have lawn despite them being on it a lot of the time.

Coll's Snapshots

Chapter Twelve

I Have to Share…

I couldn't resist adding this chapter. Over the years I have built up a collection of my favourite chicken stories and photos. Some of our more colourful characters and my observations of just how intelligent and intuitive chickens can be.

Tyler

When we moved into one of our homes, we inherited a flock of about 8 Isa Browns. These girls had been restrained to the enclosed run and were feeling a little bit neglected. Feather pecking was rife in the flock, as they battled for much-needed protein not found in their surroundings, which was dirt only. No vegetation was available. Our hearts went out to these girls straight away, so we set about making a safe area for them to free range.

The saddest of them all was a girl we called Tyler. At the time, we were watching a trashy American reality program and the main character was a vicious woman called Tyler. Now, this little sad case was a nasty piece of work. Another chicken only had to come within 2 feet of her and she'd attack them. Her aggression was ironic, as she was by far the most feather pecked of them all. Her tail consisted of only two long feathers, the rest of the area looked like she belonged in the frozen section of the supermarket.

As they began to free range, they stopped attacking each other, however, Tyler's attitude remained. Strangely, she was the most social of all the girls, and as we got to know them, she started taking to joining us on the outdoor table for a cuppa. Yes, she would literally drink from our mug. She was also very fond of attempting to take a cigarette butt left in my partners ashtray. To us, the picture of Tyler smoking and having a raspy voice just fit the bill perfectly!

As time went by, Tyler's 'hairdo' flourished, and we noted with approval that she also seemed to acquire some very nice looking natural sunlight highlights. Before long, she was by the fattest and healthiest looking of all the girls. I'm sure a lot can be said for her tea and coffee diet. However, I can't say that her attitude softened. She would still launch herself at the other ladies, and vied for the attention of the rooster in the most unladylike manner. Sadly Tyler literally laid herself to death, as most commercial layers do. I found her on her nest, her last egg underneath her. I'm sure her last word was a profanity.

The Anna's

I spent a lot of time attending local chicken auctions, and while there were many gorgeous healthy birds there, it's also the clearing ground for bird owners deem suited for nothing better than the pot. I often came home with a variety of sad sacks, including twenty Isa's from a battery farm that cost me a dollar each. I managed to rehome all of them.

One particular day, three Anacona's caught my eye. I hadn't started breeding them at that stage, and their gorgeous black with white spot plumage caught my eye. The girls were old, you could tell by the colouring of their combs and legs. I decided that they should retire on my farm, so in the back of the ute they went.

I had a lovely coop ready for them and did the usual 'keep them in there for a week' to ensure they knew where home was when I let them out. These girls weren't having a bar of captivity. I found them on the first night in the tree nearby. Worried that a fox would get them, my family and I spent a very cold evening trying to catch them to put them back in their warm home. We managed to, but the next evening, they were back in the tree. I then kept them locked away for a few more days, hoping to convince them that the cosy sleeping area warmed with hay was far nicer than the less than zero sleeping conditions found in the tree.

No luck. The Anna's (they were identical, so individual names seemed pointless) roosted high enough in the tree that I decided to let them be. They lived in the tree the whole time we lived on the farm. The challenge was finding their eggs, as they also decided a laying box was too confined. I tried placing one under the tree, but they preferred the loose dirt at the back of my shed.

Ignathio

I purchased a trio of Australorp's very early in my breeding days. I was fortunate enough to find show birds for sale by a lady who was moving interstate. Well, I have never, even to this day, seen a specimen of such finery as my leading man—Ignathio. (Mexican/Spanish names became the theme for all my boys) Iggy (for short) was a gentle giant, and I do mean giant. My partner picked him up for me while I was at work, and directed me to the coop Iggy had been put in. It was my 'holding coop', so it wasn't very person friendly in that you couldn't stand up inside it.

So, double over, I entered and came face to face with this massive boy. I have never been afraid of a rooster—until I met Iggy. I took one look at the size of his spurs, noted my vulnerable position, and was afraid. However, I had to catch him to move him to his permanent house.

My concern that was that when I went to catch his girls, they would carry on and it would cause him to do his job—protect them. So I went for him first. I needn't have bothered. He was like a baby chick when I caught him. He weighed a tonne, but he was the most gentlest boy ever.

Iggy took his role as protector very seriously, not just for his girls, but for all the ladies on the farm. Also for the rather err ... effeminate Silky Rooster we had at one stage. The moment an overhead bird screeched, Iggy was out like a shot shooing his ladies underneath the safety of trees. I also witnessed him challenge my dogs when they got too close.

However, Iggy was not altogether unaware that he was indeed the 'stud' of the farm. On occasional evenings at lock up time I'd find him down in the Isa henhouse, perched happily surrounded by a sea of red. (the perch sagging well and truly from the sheer weight of the big boy mind you!) We used to imagine his two wives waiting angrily for him in their henhouse, saying very unkind things about him and the 'hussy's' down the hill in number two. At first I would retrieve Iggy, very aware of his prize manhood not being put to good pure breeding use. One morning after doing so I noted that he was on the floor in his house, instead of his usual position next to his wives on the perch. Someone was sent to the doghouse for the night for his roaming ways I think!

My Girls

My lovely gorgeous Isa Browns were always just as important to me as all my expensive show breeds. I have to say, Isa's/Hylines are by far, in my experience, the most friendliest and social of all the breeds. Leaving external doors open in summer became difficult as the ladies would often stop by, uninvited and help themselves. One even laid her egg on our breakfast bar—thought she'd save us the trip to the henhouse perhaps! Here are a couple of my favourites photo's of my 'Red Girls'.

Glossary of Chicken Terms

Bantam. A miniature chicken, about one-fourth to one-half the size of a regular-sized chicken.

Beak. The hard, protruding portion of a bird's mouth, consisting of an upper beak and a lower beak.

Beard. The feathers (always found in association with a muff) bunched under the beaks of such breeds as Faverolle.

Bedding. Straw, wood shavings, shredded paper, or anything else scattered on the floor of a chicken coop to absorb moisture and manure.

Bloom. The moist, protective coating on a freshly laid egg that dries so fast you rarely see it.

Breed. A group of chickens that are like each other and different from other groups or pairing a rooster and hen for the purpose of obtaining fertile eggs.

Breeders. Mature chickens from which fertile eggs are collected or a person who manages chickens.

Broiler. A young tender meat chicken; also called a 'fryer'.

Brood. To care for a batch of chicks. Or the chicks themselves.

Brooder. A heated enclosure used to imitate the warmth and protection a mother hen gives her chicks.

Broody. A hen that covers eggs to warm and hatch them. Sometimes refers to a hen that stays in the nest for an extended period without producing eggs. www.backyardchickens.com/LC-glossary.html

Candle. To examine the contents of an intact egg with a strong light source.

Candler. A device that uses strong light to examine the contents of an egg.

Cannibalism. The bad habit chickens have of eating each other's flesh, feathers or eggs.

Cape. The narrow feathers between a chicken's neck and back.

Chalazae. Two white cords on each side of a yolk that keep the yolk properly positioned within the egg white; singular: chalaza.

Cloaca. The chamber just inside the vent where the digestive, reproductive and excretory tracts come together.

Clutch. A batch of eggs that are hatched together, either in a nest or in an incubator.

Coccidiosis. A parasitic protozoal infestation, usually occurring in damp, unclean housing conditions.

Cock. A male chicken; also called a 'rooster'.

Cockerel. A male chicken under one year old.

Comb. The fleshy, usually red, crown on top of a chicken's head.

Coop. The house or cage in which a chicken lives.

Crest. A puff of feathers on the heads of breeds such as Silkie or Polish; also called a 'topknot'.

Crop. A pouch at the base of a chicken's neck that bulges after the bird has eaten.

Crossbreed. The offspring of a hen and a rooster of two different breeds.

Cushion: The area of the back in front of the tail on the female chicken.

Debeak. To remove a portion of a bird's top beak to prevent cannibalism or self-pecking.

Down. The soft, fur-like fluff covering a newly hatched chick; also, the fluffy part near the bottom of any feather.

Dust bath. Chickens love to bathe in dry dust or sand and it helps remove any mites from their feathers.

Embryo. A fertilised egg at any stage of development prior to hatching.

Exhibition breeds. Chickens kept and shown for their beauty rather than their ability to lay eggs or produce meat.

Fertile. Capable of producing a chick.

Fertilised. Containing sperm.

Flock. A group of chickens living together.

Forced-air incubator. A mechanical device for hatching fertile eggs that has a fan to circulate warm air.

Fowl. Domesticated birds raised for food.

Free range. To allow chickens to roam a yard or pasture at will.

Gizzard. An organ that contains grit for grinding up the grain and plant fiber a chicken eats.

Grit. Sand and small pebbles eaten by a chicken and used by its gizzard to grind up grain and plant fibre.

Growers. Growing chickens between seven and 16 weeks.

Hackles. A rooster's cape feathers.

Hatch. The process by which a chick comes out of the egg.

Hen. A mature female chicken more than 12 months of age.

Hybrid. The offspring of a hen and rooster of different breeds, each of which might themselves be crossbred.

Impaction. Blockage of a body passage or cavity, such as the crop or cloaca.

Incubate. To maintain favorable conditions for hatching fertile eggs.

Incubation period. The time it takes for the egg to hatch, normally about 21 days.

Incubator. A mechanical device for hatching fertile eggs.

Keel. The breastbone, which resembles the keel of a boat.

Litter. Straw, wood shavings, shredded paper, or anything else scattered on the floor of a chicken coop, run or brooder to absorb moisture and manure.

Mite. A tiny jointed-legged body parasite.
Moult. The annual shedding and renewing of a bird's feathers.

Nest box. A secluded safe place where a hen feels she can leave her eggs.
Nest egg. A wooden or plastic egg put in the nest box to encourage hens to lay there.

Oviduct. The tube inside a hen through which an egg travels when it is ready to be laid.

Pasting. Loose droppings sticking to vent area, also known as 'pasting up' and 'sticky bottoms'.
Pecking order. The social ranking of a flock—they figure it out by size and temperament. There really is a 'pecking order' and you will soon be able to tell by watching your chickens.
Pellets. Poultry pellets are formed from a fine mash bonded together.
Perch. The place where chickens sleep at night; the act of resting on a perch; also called a 'roost'.

Pigmentation. The color of a chicken's beak, shanks and vent.

Pinfeathers. The tips of newly emerging feathers.

Pip. The hole a newly formed chick makes in its shell when it is ready to hatch.

Plumage. The total set of feathers covering a chicken.

Point of lay: The age at which a bird could start laying (approx. 24 weeks).

Poultry. Domestic fowls, such as chickens, turkeys, ducks, or geese, raised for meat or eggs.

Pullet. A female chicken under one year old.

Purebred. The offspring of a hen and rooster of the same breed.

Roost. The place where chickens spend the night; the act of resting on a roost; also called a 'perch'.

Rooster. A male chicken; also called a 'cock'.

Saddle. The part of a chicken's back just before the tail.

Scales. The small, hard overlapping plates covering a chicken's shanks and toes.

Sexed. Newly hatched chicks that have been sorted into pullets and cockerels.

Sex feather. A hackle, saddle, or tail feather that is rounded in a hen but usually pointed in a rooster (except in breeds that are hen feathered).

Sex linking. Any inherited factor linked to sex chromosomes. This allows the visual identification of gender in day-old chicks—typically by plumage colour difference between males and females.

Shank. The part of a chicken's leg between the claw and the first joint.

Sickles. The long, curved tail feathers of some roosters.

Spurs. The sharp pointed protrusions on a rooster's shanks.

Started pullets. Young female chickens that are nearly old enough to lay.

Starter. A feed ration for newly hatched chicks, also called 'crumbles'.

Sternum. Breastbone or keel.

Stub. Down on the shank or toe of a clean-legged chicken.

Trachea. Windpipe.

Variety. Subdivision of a breed according to color, comb style, beard or leg feathering.

Vent. The outside opening of the cloaca, through which a chicken emits eggs and droppings from separate channels.

Wattles. The two red or purplish flaps of flesh that dangle under a chicken's chin.

Resources

Online Poultry Forums

Backyard Poultry – www.backyardpoultry.com.au

Australian Poultry Forum – www.australianpoultryforum. com.

'Chooknet'–www.chooknet.com.au"www.chooknet.com.au

Backyard Chickens (American) –

www.backyardchickens.com"www.backyardchickens.com

www.practiclepoultry.co.uk (UK)

www.forums.thepoultryKeeper.co.uk (UK)

www.backyardpoultrymag.com (USA)

Magazines

Australiasian Poultry (AU)

Backyard Poultry (USA)

Practical Poultry (UK)

Specialist Poultry Suppliers

Large range of incubators, brooders, etc. Online ordering facility.

www.wapoultryequipment.net.au/

www.tkpoultrysupplies.com.au

Backyard Chickens Blog

www.chicksinthecity.com.au

Appendix — Breed List

/pw = per week

Breed	Size	Eggs	Personality
Ameraucana (USA) — also referred to as an 'Easter Egger'	Med	3–4/pw blue/green/cream	Calm and good with children
Ancona	Med	5/pw large white	Flighty, nervous
Araucana	Small	3/pw med blue	Calm and friendly
Australorp (AU)	Heavy	5/pw large brown	Friendly and docile, perfect around children. Rarely attempts to fly.
Barnevelder	Med	3/pw large brown	Mild and placid
Belgian D'Uccle	Bantam	2/pw tiny cream	Mild temperament, rarely aggressive
Black Star (USA) Hybrid	Med	5/pw med brown	Excellent backyard layer with lovely temperament
Faverolle	Heavy	4/pw med cream	Mild and placid
Frizzle	Bantam	3/pw small Brown	Friendly and interactive

Breed	Size	Eggs	Personality
Isa/Hyline Brown*	Med	6–7/pw large cream	Friendly, curious and placid
Leghorn	Heavy	5–6/pw large white	Shy and flighty
Maran	Heavy	3/pw large dark brown	Friendly and very active
New Hampshire	Heavy	3/pw large brown	Friendly and curious, but roosters can be aggressive
Orpington	Heavy	3/pw large brown	Friendly and sweet, love a good cuddle
Pekin Bantams	Bantam (Heavy)	2/pw small brown	Friendly balls of fluff, good mothers
Plymouth Rock	Heavy	4/pw large brown	Friendly and calm
Polish Crested	Small	2/pw tiny white	Friendly and interesting appearance
Rhode Island Red	Heavy	5/pw X-large brown	Full of personality and love people. Roosters can be aggressive
Silkie	Bantam	3/pw tiny cream	Docile and friendly, great with children

Breed	Size	Eggs	Personality
Sussex—light	Heavy	4/pw large light brown	Lovely pets, don't mind being held and will interact with people.
Sussex— Speckled	Heavy	4/pw large light brown	As per Light Sussex
Welsummer	Medium	3/pw large dark brown	Friendly and active
Wyandotte— Silver Laced	Heavy	4/pw large brown	Can become aggressive
Wyandotte – Gold Laced	Heavy	4/pw large brown	As per Silver Laced

About the Author

Michelle has grown up with chickens and turned her passion into a small hobby farm business. During this time she spread the joy of owning chickens into suburban backyards and local schools. Now based on a 500-square metre block, Michelle, her partner, and son still enjoy the benefits of feathered friends—albeit a much smaller flock!

UK £9.99
US $12.99